Old ASTON, ERDINGTON, KINGSTANDING, AND

by
Eric Armstrong

Lively entertainment was provided either side of the Bartons Arms (centre). The domed building on the left was The Globe Electric Palace, an early picture house opened in 1913, closed c.1955 and subsequently demolished; the building to the right, with its billboard facing the camera, was the Aston Hippodrome. Will Hay, listed on the advert as appearing at the music hall, was a comedian who later starred in a number of comedy films including 'Convict 99' and 'Oh, Mr Porter!' The 'Aston Hipp' (now demolished) enjoyed a somewhat raffish reputation and was very well patronised. Cinemas such as The Globe were often known as 'flea-pits', although this was a term of affection rather than condemnation.

1

THE OLD CROSS, ASTON.

First published in the United Kingdom, 1999,
by Stenlake Publishing Ltd.
01290 551122
www.stenlake.co.uk
ISBN 9781840330762
Printed by Blissetts, Roslin Road, Acton, W3 8DH

The publishers regret that they cannot supply copies of any pictures featured in this book

FURTHER READING

The books listed below were used by the author during his research. None of them are available from Stenlake Publishing. Those interested in finding out more are advised to contact their local bookshop or reference library.

Birmingham on Old Postcards, John Marks; Vol. 1, 1982; Vol. 2, 1983; Vol. 3, 1990; Reflections of a Bygone Age.

The Dream Palaces of Birmingham, Chris & Rosemary Clegg, Published by the authors, 1983.

Aston Villa, A Portrait in Old Picture Postcards, Derrick Spinks, S.B. Publications, 1991.

Up The Terrace Down Aston and Lozells, Ronald K. Moore, Westwood Press Publications, 1988, Reprinted 1993.

The Story of Erdington, Douglas V. Jones, Westwood Press Publications, 5th impression, 1995.

Memories of a Twenties Child, Douglas V. Jones, Westwood Press Publications, 1981, 2nd impression 1988.

Growing Up and Ducking Down, Eric Armstrong, Minerva Press, 1997. (Available from bookshops priced £6.99 Please quote ISBN 1 86106 275 3.)

Excerpts from the author's schoolboy diaries for 1938, 1939, and 1940 have been included in this book where relevant.

Branching away from High Street is park lane, at the end of which was the well-known site of Aston Cross. The old cross marked the entrance to the private estates of a notable family of landed gentry called the Holtes, whose history is bound up with that of Aston Hall (see page 12).

Six Ways, Aston is a better place than many from which to begin an exploration of the suburbs covered by this book. The steam tram (made up of a locomotive with a tall funnel, towing the double decker passenger vehicle behind it) has laboured, at less than 15 m.p.h., up Birchfield Road before entering High Street, Aston on its lumbering way to the city centre. Running left and right of Christ Church Baptist Chapel are Witton Road and Victoria Road. The entrance to Lozells Road is on the right of the lamp-post and branching away right at the bollards is the unseen Alma Street, making six ways in all. The sender of the postcard (March 26, 1907) comments: 'Electric trams have only been running since last Xmas'. Ogden's were a large manufacturer of cigarettes based in Liverpool.

The products of a major Aston company on display at what is presumed to be a trade fair. Aston was the largest and most populous of the parishes to be incorporated into Birmingham in 1911, and was also a heavily industrialised area.

Travelling away from the city centre, Lichfield Road leads to the Staffordshire cathedral town of Lichfield via Erdington and Sutton Coldfield. Many corner shops and hucksters' shops (which occupied partly-converted dwelling houses) lined stretches of this long road. Above the second awning on the left an HP advert can be identified, with one letter either side of the sauce bottle. Trams passed with minimal clearance beneath the bridge of Aston railway station.

Victoria Road, Aston.

Victoria Road is another spoke from the hub of Six Ways, Aston. The suburb's public swimming baths (right) housed two pools, charging 6d for first class amenities and 4d for second in the late 1920s. The first class pool was blue in colour and the second class of a greenish hue, the difference in colour perhaps designed to mark a distinction between them. Slipper baths were also available, and as many Aston homes lacked a bathroom, these baths, providing 'a good hot tub', were popular, especially at weekends.

Trinity Road

Witton Road, another of the Six Ways thoroughfares, crossed Trinity Road before reaching the area known as Witton. The higher part of Trinity Road, shown here, consisted of fine residential property. Villa Park, home of the 'claret and blues', was a few minutes walk away.

A No. 3 tram (Witton and Six Ways) at its Witton Terminus in 1937. Belisha beacons were in widespread use by this time. *28 October 1938. Dennis told me this afternoon that she (Margaret) says meet me at half 6 at island, Witton.* The date was kept, near the shops with the awnings which bear the legend 'Birmingham Co-operative Society'. Part of the island can just be made out, on the right, and the two 'sweethearts', age 15 and 14, went on to enjoy a wonderful evening at the Onion Fair held on the nearby Serpentine ground. The Onion Fair owed its origins to Birmingham's Michaelmas Fair which dated back to the fifteenth century. Held traditionally in the Bull Ring, the fair eventually moved to Aston and was renamed (although no one knows quite why it became the Onion Fair). The fair ceased to be held some thirty years ago.

A line of trams wait in Trinity Road for the full-time whistle to blow at Villa Park on Saturday 10 September 1949. Part of the Trinity Road stand is visible behind the last tram. Seated on the steps of the third car, the driver and conductor (presumably) are enjoying a mug of tea. The overhanging trees are growing in Aston Park.

ASTON VILLA FOOTBALL GROUND, BIRMINGHAM

This picture, taken from the terraces at the Witton end, is reproduced from a postcard thought to date from around 1904. Aston village players are wearing white knicks and their opponents black. The stripes on the original colour postcard appear to be red and white, so the visiting team might have been Sheffield United, Sunderland, Southampton or Lincoln City. Around the perimeter of the grassed area runs a concrete, banked cycling track. The high hoarding to the right was designed to prevent miserly, hard-up or casual supporters from watching the game buckshee from the slopes of Aston Park.

'Meet you in the Holte before kick-off'. The Holte Hotel, a Mitchells and Butlers house, was a popular pre-match rendezvous, situated at the junction of Trinity Road with Witton Lane. The edge of Aston Park stretches away to the left.

Aston Hall is a Jacobean mansion dating back to the early seventeenth century. It was the home of Sir Thomas Holte, 'cock of the walk' in the rural Aston of his day. During the English Civil War, the hall was bombarded and besieged by Roundhead troops and after a few days of fighting this Royalist stronghold was captured. The damage done by cannon balls remains a feature for tourist visitors. The corporation of Birmingham acquired the house in 1863. Its gardens became a public park and it was here that Birmingham staged a week-long pageant to celebrate its centenary as a city during July 1938.

A winsome urchin, photographed, according to a pencilled note on the postcard, in Aston Park. The presence of puddles and an open umbrella to the right suggest a recent shower. The card is postmarked 1915.

Left: This large, almost cathedral-sized church with its lofty spire is Aston parish church. It stands close to the north-east corner of Aston Park.

Aston Church from the Park Gates

Right: A self-explanatory symbol of remembrance. Many Birmingham men served in the Royal Warwickshire Regiment during World War I. It was with this regiment that the future Field Marshal Mongomery (Monty of Alamein) served.

ITALY

FRANCE   BELGIUM

TO THE
GLORIOUS MEMORY
OF THE
OFFICERS WARRANT OFFICERS
NON-COMMISSIONED OFFICERS
AND MEN OF THE
8TH BATTALION
THE ROYAL WARWICKSHIRE
REGIMENT
WHO LAID DOWN THEIR LIVES IN
THE GREAT WAR
1914 — 1919

CENOTAPH ASTON

GRAMMAR SCHOOL ALBERT RD
ASTON

King Edward's Grammar School for Boys, on the southern edge of Aston Park. As a school, its only drawback (in the compiler's view when a boy) was that it gave itself airs by having its boys play rugger instead of proper soccer football.

Frederick Road, Aston.

Frederick Road runs parallel with the southern boundary of Aston Park, and is typical of some of the more upmarket residential streets of Aston. The small front gardens, bordered by low brick walls and iron railings, the bay windows and a porch or two, are all indicative of a certain respectability.

United We Stand 1915

KYNOCH

12

Birmingham "Win the War" Day, September 21st 1918

Despite not having a distinctive centre, Witton was well-known to most people for Village Park, the Onion Fair and the many jobs provided by its large factories. 'Oh, he works at the GEC, Witton' one neighbour might say to another. The compiler's mother worked, with her sister, 'on munitions' at Kynoch's during World War I. Their three brothers all became long service employees at this factory, although its ownership later changed several times (the present owner is IMI). Win The War Day was probably a morale-boosting exercise designed to raise the spirits of key workers (such as these munitions workers), who were of vital importance to the war effort. A companion postcard shows a bevy of factory girls sitting around a display of shell cases.

Something of the monotony and discipline of factory work is suggested by the writer of this card of Kynoch's works, '. . . sending you this picture of that unique building containing the clock which is Greenwich to father'. This is probably a reference to the strict ritual of 'clocking on' for factory workers. A factory rule, understandable given Kynoch's involvement with explosives, read:'No matches are allowed inside the works. Anyone having them in their possession must hand them to the gatekeeper.'

G.239.

BROOK VALE PARK, ERDINGTON. (54)

Moving away from Witton in a north-easterly direction, the number 11 bus, (the Outer Circle service, introduced in 1926) trundled along Brookvale Road, past the vast Witton cemetery, before passing Witton Lakes to its left and Brookvale Park with its extensive lake to the right. The lake served as a reservoir until Birmingham tapped into a new source of water from the Elan Valley in Wales in 1904. King Edward VII performed the opening ceremony on 21 July.

Stockland Hotel, Stockland Green.

Continuing in the same direction, the number 11 bus reached the newer residential area of Stockland Green. The modern and spacious Stockland Green Hotel with its large car park was typical of the less congested suburbs. The awning over the corner shop carries the name 'George Baines', a noted Birmingham baker. Having crossed the tramlines the Outer Circle service travelled up Reservoir Road to another hub with six spokes, Six Ways, Erdington. This card was posted in 1944.

SIX WAYS, ERDINGTON. (48)

G.230.

Reservoir Road enters from the left by 'Archer's Supply Stores'. The people at the barrier are waiting for a tram to come down High Street to take them towards Gravelly Hill, in the direction of the city centre. The traffic island was one of the first to be installed in England.

Gravelly Hill, one of the approach roads to Six Ways, Erdington, and an extension of Lichfield Road. The sheep appear to be well under control, but what happened when a tram came along? One can just be made out in front of the church.)

KINGSBURY RD ERDINGTON

Kingsbury Road, with its substantial residential property, bears right from the church shown in the picture opposite. This postcard is dated 22 May 1922. Centuries ago, Erdington was a tiny hamlet within the very extensive parish of Aston. In 1894, having grown substantially, it became an urban district, with administrative offices located in Kingsbury Road. In 1911 Erdington became part of Birmingham.

HIGH STREET, ERDINGTON   85387 JV

Trams had to operate on a single track through this narrow section of High Street, Erdington, the centre of the old village. The card was posted on 14 July 1924.

THE GREEN, ERDINGTON. (50)

The vestigial remains of Erdington Green, originally a pukka village green, form a small triangle adjacent to the parked cards on the right of the picture.

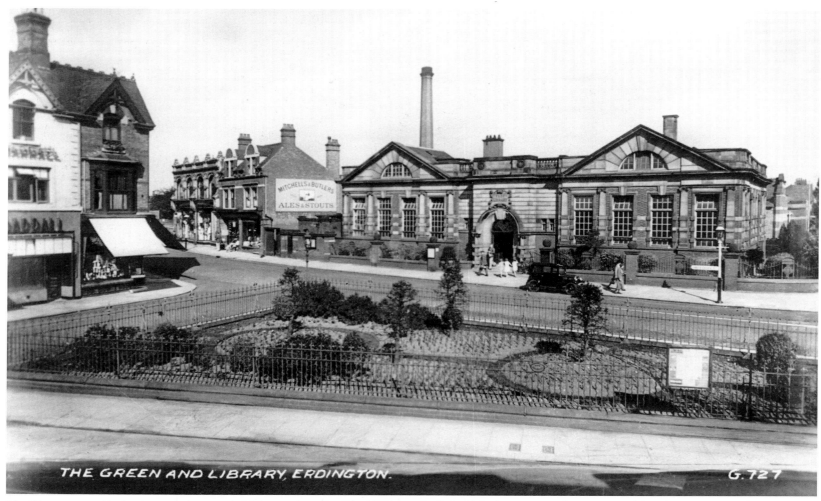

THE GREEN AND LIBRARY, ERDINGTON.   G.727

The library opposite the truncated green (which was fenced off in 1887) was built in 1907. It was one of a number of free libraries created through the generosity of Andrew Carnegie, the Scottish/American millionaire and philanthropist who endowed a fund for the creation of provincial library services. A familiar and prominent West Midlands brewery advertisement is visible close by, reading 'Mitchells and Butlers Ales and Stouts', with the famous 'deer's leap' picture in the centre of the advert.

26

SUTTON NEW ROAD, ERDINGTON

During 1938, a bypass in Erdington village was completed which diverted traffic from the High Street. Named Sutton New Road, it provided tram tracks along a central reservation.

The first TRAM in ERDINGTON 1.3.07.

31 years earlier, before the building of the Sutton New Road (previous picture), the position was somewhat different! The tram's destination is Steelhouse Lane in Birmingham city centre. At the inauguration gentlemen (mostly bowler hatted) apparently preferred to travel upstairs, leaving one rather forlorn-looking lady downstairs on what seems to be a raw March day.

The message on the back of this card reads 'Erdington Cottage Homes children going for a trip at Rhyl'. From the style of the hats and the girls' gymslips the photograph probably dates from the late 1920s. Rhyl, a north Wales coastal resort, was a popular destination with Birmingham people travelling on coach day trips. Here, however, the girls appear to be having a 'chara' outing during a holiday in Rhyl. The vehicle certainly points up the derivation of the word charabanc—a car with benches. Note its speed, bottom left-hand corner—12 m.p.h.!

29

2642 JAFFRAY HOSPITAL ERDINGTON

This country house style hospital, now demolished, was opened by the Prince of Wales (the future King Edward VII) well before Erdington became part of Birmingham. John Jaffray (1818-1901) was a Scotsman who moved to Birmingham where he became a journalist for, and eventually a partner in, a Birmingham newspaper. He prospered and engaged in philanthropic activities including the building of this hospital which opened in 1885. Jaffray was knighted for his public services.

PYPE HAYES PARK & HALL,
ERDINGTON, BIRMINGHAM.

Adjacent to Erdington in an easterly direction lies an area known as Pype Hayes. Pype Hayes Hall, dating back to the seventeenth century, was built and long occupied by the Bagot family. In 1919, the hall became the property of Birmingham Corporation, first serving as a convalescent home. After the Second World War it housed a children's residential nursery and is currently used for offices. The estate grounds became a public park, which included a municipal golf course.

TYBURN RD. PYPE HAYES   ERDINGTON

A constant stream of cars and lorries now thunders along the dual carriageway of Tyburn Road, south-west of Pype Hayes Hall and Park. The tram routes were designed to ferry Dunlop workers to and from the giant new factory which in 1916 replaced the old one at Aston Cross. Before the tram service became available, the company arranged for its workers to be transported by canal boats to and from Aston.

When Irish veterinary surgeon John Boyd Dunlop (1840–1921) began experimenting on his son's tricycle, he could hardly have imagined that his eventual development of the pneumatic tyre could lead to the growth of such an enormous business. The massive Fort Dunlop was built on what was essentially a rural site close to the Tyburn Road. In the bottom left-hand corner a fenced bend of cut grassland is visible. This probably formed part of Bromford Bridge racecourse which, between the wars, was popular with the horse-racing fraternity. *8 October 1938. Had a good pair of Dunlop pumps. 5/11.* Dunlop denoted quality!

A tranquil scene from 1928. This section of Chester Road once formed part of the route for stagecoaches which plied between London and Chester. Nowadays commuter and juggernaut traffic makes its deafening way along here to or from the motorway network.

OSCOTT COLLEGE, SUTTON COLDFIELD, BIRMINGHAM.

Oscott College, a Roman Catholic theological college set in extensive grounds, stands in an elevated position further to the north-west, also on Chester Road. This well-appointed building was designed by A.W.N. Pugin, a noted architect of many Catholic churches. The college continues to carry out its original purpose.

HANDSWORTH WOOD ROAD

Birchfield Road runs virtually due north from Six Ways, Aston, through Perry Barr, Great Barr and on to Walsall. By branching away at appropriate points, the suburbs of Handsworth, Hamstead, and Kingstanding can be reached. This picture of Handsworth Wood Road, with its tree-lined pavements and substantial houses, is indicative of comfortable prosperity. Cramped, huddled, colliers' cottages and the hazards of coal mining lay only a mile ahead in the pit village of Hamstead.

THE MINERS' LAST MESSAGE.

Hamstead Colliery began producing coal in 1880. On 4 March 1908, fire broke out below ground leaving a number of miners trapped. Local rescue attempts proved unsuccessful, so the aid of a special rescue team (Normanton and Barnsley) was called upon. Sadly, their efforts also failed, and one of the team, John Welsby, died, overcome by fumes. Eventually 25 bodies were recovered. 76 pit ponies also died.

The poignant last message, chalked on a door, of one of the miners who lost his life.

High Bridges, Great Barr.

382-5.

Running over this bridge formed part of Handsworth Grammar School's annual cross country race. *16 March 1938. Cross Country today. Came 5th. 22 March 1939. Managed to struggle in 4th.* High hopes as well as High Bridges!

429/18.

Barr Beacon.

The semi-rural nature of the outer edge of Great Barr. Large bonfires were lit on Barr Beacon, a public open space, to mark major celebratory occasions such as the end of World War I.

"SCOTT" SERIES, No. 1093

Tram Terminus, PERRY BARR.

Back to Birchfield Road and a steam tram (made up of a locomotive towing a separate passenger vehicle) which advertises knife polish and a Nestle's product. The message on the back of the card reads: 'Birmingham's motto is forward (note tram). You have <u>now</u> got one in Manchester. Fancy the Villa losing on Sat. There must have been an accident somewhere . . .'

Rumbling away from Perry barr, the open top bus is travelling in the Great Barr and Walsall direction and has just crossed the bridge over the River Tame. The area on the right became the site of a 1930s housing development and Perry hall Playing Fields. The spire of Christ's Church, at the corner of Aldridge Road, is visible in the distance.

WALSALL RD. PERRY BARR

The turning on the left marks the entrance to Perry Avenue, which provided access to Perry Hall Playing Fields (named after Perry Hall which formerly stood nearby). The KEEP LEFT sign stands in Church Road, from where there was an entrance into Perry Park. Great Barr lies directly ahead. The card was posted in May 1938.

THE TWO BRIDGES, PERRY BARR.

Returning to Perry Barr and moving into Aldridge Road, traffic eventually crossed over the River Tame by means of a new bridge running parallel with the historic Zig Zag bridge. The card, posted in 1937, shows the bridge in its pristine white glory. Additional bus routes were established as new council estates, notably Kingstanding, developed.

PERRY VILLAGE AND CHURCH.

A little further along Aldridge Road, at the junction with Church Road, stands a newer type of corner shop with brick and pebble-dash walls. The tower of St John's Church, Church Road, can be seen in the distance. To the right, but not visible, is another entrance to Perry Park. The postcard was sent in 12 September 1926.

KINGSTANDING RD.

The 1930s saw the building of many new houses, particularly through the creation of extensive council estates. In areas of north Birmingham rapid expansion took place in Kingstanding, Perry Common and Pheasey. It is commonly claimed that Kingstanding derived its name from the occasion when King Charles I addressed local Royalist supporters from a modest hilltop there, early during the English Civil War (1642). Postmarked 1939, this card gives a good impression of the fine dual carriageway, a mile-and-a-half or so in length, running from College Road to the six ways ('The Circle') at the heart of Kingstanding Estate.

This card of The Circle was posted in 1935. Silhouetted to the right of the central path stands a slender column, bearing the clock where bus drivers clocked on at the terminus.

Sent on 16 June 1933, this card of King's Road features another spacious new dual carriageway, this time connecting Queslett Road with Chester Road. The road is about a mile-and-a-half long and completely straight, except for where The Circle intervenes.

Large pubs became fashionable on the new, spacious council estates, and the style of this one could perhaps be described as '1930s Mock Baronial'! The aristocratic theme was continued on the inn sign; the rider of the white charger was presumably meant to represent King Charles I. The card is postmarked 10 August 1936. A few months later King Edward VIII abdicated.